MOJANG

DEL REY
NEW YORK

Published in the United States by Del Rey, an imprint of Random House, a division of Penguin Random House LLC, New York.

DEL REY and the HOUSE colophon are registered trademarks of Penguin Random House LLC.

Published in hardcover in the United Kingdom by Egmont UK Limited.

Written by Stephanie Milton. Additional material by Marsh Davies and Owen Jones.

Illustrations by Ryan Marsh

ISBN 978-0-399-18201-3
Ebook ISBN 978-1-5247-9740-9

Printed in China on acid-free paper by C & C Offset

randomhousebooks.com

4 6 8 9 7 5

Design by Andrea Philpots and John Stuckey

GUIDE TO:
↗EXPLORATION

CONTENTS

1. THE MINECRAFT LANDSCAPE

2. MOBS

3. SURVIVAL

INTRODUCTION

Welcome to the official Guide to Exploration! Since Survival mode was added to Minecraft, players around the world have gone on millions of exciting adventures. Though it's fun to play with infinite resources in Creative mode, there's something special about building things out of hard-won materials harvested from your Minecraft world. I think it's the most satisfying way to play.

We've packed this guide with hints and tips gathered from years of experience. You'll learn about the different biomes waiting to be discovered and what you might find in each one, the mobs you'll encounter on your journey, and some of the vital items you'll need to survive and thrive.

Be brave and enjoy exploring!

OWEN JONES
THE MOJANG TEAM

THE TECHNICAL STUFF

Before you start your first game there are some decisions to make about how you'd like to play. This page will help you decide whether you'd like to venture out alone or as part of a group, and which game mode is right for you.

EDITIONS

Minecraft is available to play on several different platforms. So, however and wherever you prefer to play, there's an edition for you.

DESKTOP	**CONSOLE**	**POCKET**

 Windows

Windows 10

 Apple

 Linux

Raspberry Pi

Xbox ONE

Xbox 360

PS4

PS3

PSVITA

 WiiU

Nintendo Switch

iOS

 tv

 Android

 Windows M

kindle fire

fireTV

Gear VR

SINGLE PLAYER, MULTIPLAYER OR REALMS

Once you've chosen a platform, you can decide what kind of adventure you want to have, whether that's alone or with friends, in a new world, or in a map that's been designed by someone else.

Single player is the original, default mode for Minecraft. This mode is for you if you prefer to take on the challenges of Minecraft alone rather than in a team.

Choose multiplayer if you want to share your adventure with friends on the same network. One person will need to set up a LAN (local area network) game for the others to join.

Some editions support Minecraft Realms – a service that allows you to rent a server from Mojang. It's completely secure and safe – only people you invite can join your server.

GAME MODE

Finally, there are several different game modes to choose from, offering various degrees of difficulty.

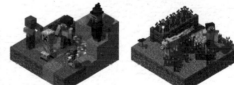

SURVIVAL

Choose Survival mode and you'll have loads of fun fighting hostile monsters and collecting materials to help you stay alive. You'll need to eat, and you'll gain experience and levels as you play.

CREATIVE

In Creative mode you're free from hostile mobs, you can fly around and destroy blocks instantly. You'll also have a full inventory of materials with which to build amazing structures.

HARDCORE

If you choose Hardcore mode, the difficulty will be locked on hard and you'll only get one life. If you die it really will be game over – your world will be deleted and you'll have to start again.

PEACEFUL

You can also choose a peaceful option in Survival mode. You'll still collect materials and craft in order to survive, but without the hostile mobs. And your health will regenerate, too.

CONTROLS

Once you've chosen an edition, use the next few pages to familiarise yourself with the basic controls. If you get stuck in the middle of a game you can refer back to these pages for help.

DESKTOP EDITION CONTROLS

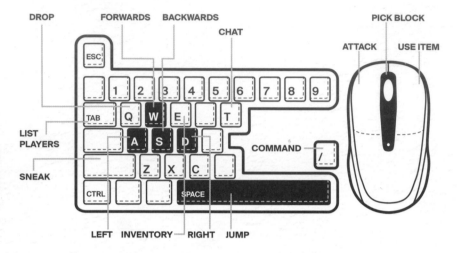

POCKET EDITION CONTROLS

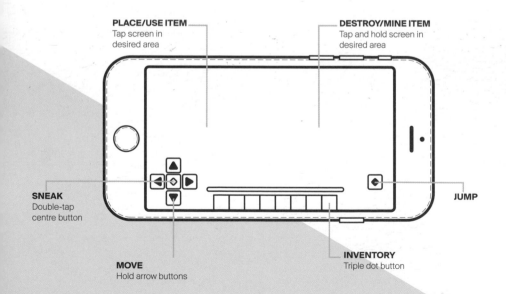

PLACE/USE ITEM
Tap screen in desired area

DESTROY/MINE ITEM
Tap and hold screen in desired area

SNEAK
Double-tap centre button

JUMP

MOVE
Hold arrow buttons

INVENTORY
Triple dot button

PLAYSTATION CONTROLS

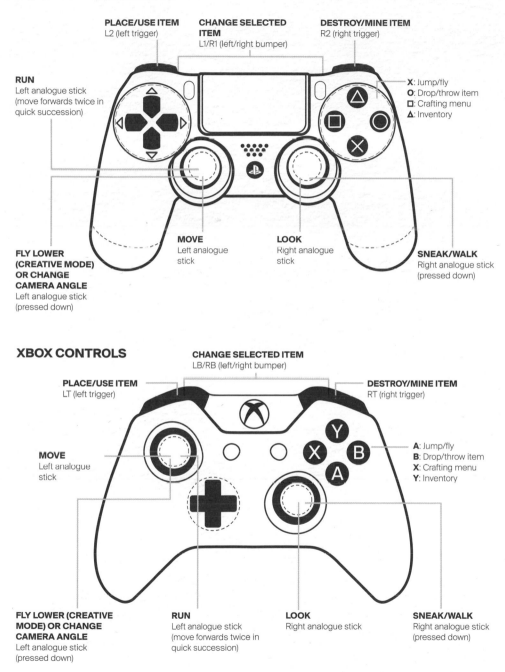

PLACE/USE ITEM
L2 (left trigger)

CHANGE SELECTED ITEM
L1/R1 (left/right bumper)

DESTROY/MINE ITEM
R2 (right trigger)

RUN
Left analogue stick
(move forwards twice in
quick succession)

X: Jump/fly
O: Drop/throw item
□: Crafting menu
△: Inventory

MOVE
Left analogue
stick

LOOK
Right analogue
stick

**FLY LOWER
(CREATIVE MODE)
OR CHANGE
CAMERA ANGLE**
Left analogue stick
(pressed down)

SNEAK/WALK
Right analogue stick
(pressed down)

XBOX CONTROLS

CHANGE SELECTED ITEM
LB/RB (left/right bumper)

PLACE/USE ITEM
LT (left trigger)

DESTROY/MINE ITEM
RT (right trigger)

MOVE
Left analogue
stick

A: Jump/fly
B: Drop/throw item
X: Crafting menu
Y: Inventory

**FLY LOWER (CREATIVE
MODE) OR CHANGE
CAMERA ANGLE**
Left analogue stick
(pressed down)

RUN
Left analogue stick
(move forwards twice in
quick succession)

LOOK
Right analogue stick

SNEAK/WALK
Right analogue stick
(pressed down)

PLAYSTATION VITA CONTROLS

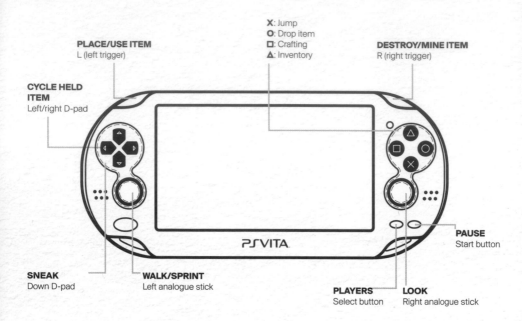

PLACE/USE ITEM
L (left trigger)

CYCLE HELD ITEM
Left/right D-pad

X: Jump
O: Drop item
□: Crafting
△: Inventory

DESTROY/MINE ITEM
R (right trigger)

SNEAK
Down D-pad

WALK/SPRINT
Left analogue stick

PLAYERS
Select button

LOOK
Right analogue stick

PAUSE
Start button

PSVITA

Wii U GAMEPAD CONTROLS

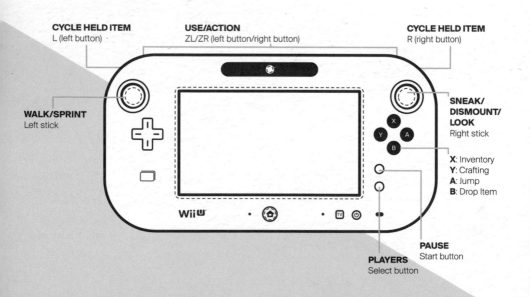

CYCLE HELD ITEM
L (left button)

USE/ACTION
ZL/ZR (left button/right button)

CYCLE HELD ITEM
R (right button)

WALK/SPRINT
Left stick

**SNEAK/
DISMOUNT/
LOOK**
Right stick

X: Inventory
Y: Crafting
A: Jump
B: Drop Item

PLAYERS
Select button

PAUSE
Start button

Wii U

INVENTORY

When you play in Survival, Hardcore or Peaceful mode you'll collect lots of useful blocks and items, which you'll need to store and manage in your inventory. You can open your inventory at any time – refer back to pages 8-10 to check how to do it on your edition.

ARMOUR SLOTS
See page 89 for instructions on how to craft and equip armour.

CRAFTING GRID
Drag materials into the crafting grid to craft simple items such as wood planks and torches.

OUTPUT SQUARE
Your newly crafted item will appear in your output square ready to put in your inventory.

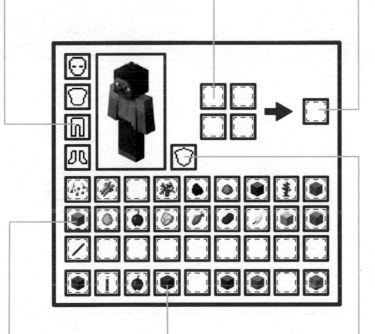

ITEM SLOTS
There are 27 item slots available. Many blocks and items can be stacked together, up to a maximum of 64. Some items, like eggs and buckets, can only be stacked up to a maximum of 16. Items like tools cannot be stacked at all. Hover over any item in your inventory and its name will appear.

HOTBAR SLOTS
Your hotbar is visible at all times. It allows you to access items quickly, without having to open your inventory and search for them. It's ideal for storing things you'll need in an emergency like weapons and food. Your main hand contains whichever item is currently selected in your hotbar.

OFF-HAND SLOT
Your off-hand slot can be equipped to hold a second item, which will enable you to dual-wield. You will automatically use the item in your off-hand slot when there is no item in your main slot. You can't use weapons when they're in your off-hand slot, but it's ideal for items like arrows, food or torches.

KEY

Throughout this book you'll see symbols that represent different items, values or properties – they cover everything from causes of damage to mob drops. Refer back to this page when you spot them to check what they mean.

GENERAL

MOJANG STUFF

This super-exclusive info has come directly from the developers at Mojang.

∞

Indicates that this item is an unlimited drop, while the mob in question is alive.

SPAWN LIGHT LEVEL

15

9

0

Indicates the light level at which a mob spawns. In this example, the mob spawns at a light level of 9 or higher.

Mob does not die when the sun rises.

HOSTILITY

Indicates the hostility level of a mob – yellow is passive, orange is neutral and red is hostile.

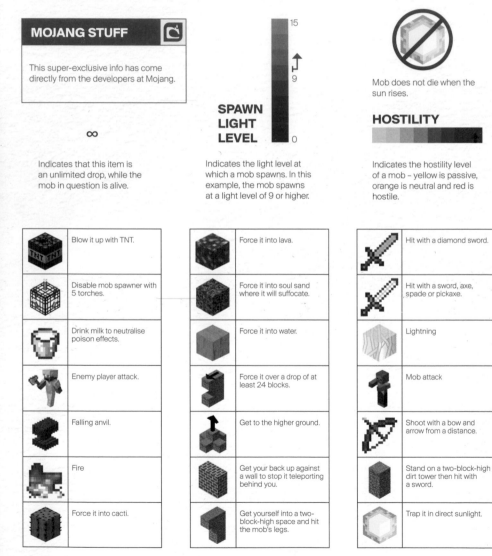

	Blow it up with TNT.		Force it into lava.		Hit with a diamond sword.
	Disable mob spawner with 5 torches.		Force it into soul sand where it will suffocate.		Hit with a sword, axe, spade or pickaxe.
	Drink milk to neutralise poison effects.		Force it into water.		Lightning
	Enemy player attack.		Force it over a drop of at least 24 blocks.		Mob attack
	Falling anvil.		Get to the higher ground.		Shoot with a bow and arrow from a distance.
	Fire		Get your back up against a wall to stop it teleporting behind you.		Stand on a two-block-high dirt tower then hit with a sword.
	Force it into cacti.		Get yourself into a two-block-high space and hit the mob's legs.		Trap it in direct sunlight.

ITEMS, BLOCKS AND EFFECTS

	Axe		Egg		Mushroom (brown)		Raw rabbit
	Armour		Emerald		Mushroom (red)		Raw salmon
	Arrow		Ender pearl		Naturally spawned equipment		Redstone
	Bone		Experience point		Paper		Roast chicken
	Bow		Feather		Picked-up equipment		Rotten flesh
	Bowl		Fireball, fire charge or ender acid ball		Potato		Saddle
	Carpet		Glass bottle		Prismarine crystal		Slimeball
	Carrot		Glowstone dust		Prismarine shard		Spider eye
	Chest		Gold ingot		Pufferfish		Steak
	Clownfish		Golden nugget		Rabbit hide		Stick
	Cooked cod		Gunpowder		Rabbit's foot		String
	Cooked mutton		Horse armour		Raw beef		Sugar
	Cooked porkchop		Ink sac		Raw chicken		Totem of undying
	Cooked rabbit		Iron ingot		Raw cod		Wet sponge
	Cooked salmon		Leather		Raw mutton		Wool
	Creeper head		Music disc		Raw porkchop		

BEFORE YOU SPAWN

This guide assumes you are playing alone in Survival mode. Before you start your first game (and 'spawn' into the world you've created), there are a few things to understand about the mysterious world of Minecraft.

WORLD SEED

This is the string of numbers or characters that generates every Minecraft world and determines what it will look like. People often share the best seeds online. The world seed is set automatically, but you can set it manually if there's a particular seed you'd like to try – go to 'create new world' then 'more world options' to enter the seed.

BLOCKS

The Minecraft landscape is made of naturally generated blocks, but you can also craft blocks yourself. Blocks can be placed on top of other blocks and used for building. Some are opaque, others transparent, and they can be liquid or solid. Many blocks also have a function, e.g. torches provide a light source and cake restores food points.

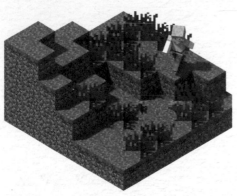

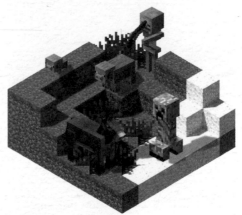

ITEMS

Items can't be placed in the Minecraft world, but can be held and dropped for other players to pick up. They generally have a function, e.g. tools, and can often be combined with other items to craft blocks, e.g. gunpowder.

MOBS

Mob is short for 'mobile' and refers to all living, moving creatures. Mobs can be passive, neutral or hostile. Some mobs are tameable, and two are categorised as utility mobs since they can help defend you.

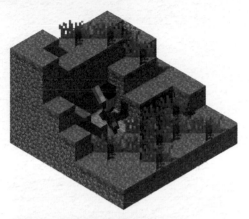

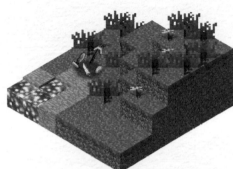

BREAKING BLOCKS

You need to break blocks to collect them. Some, e.g. wood, can be broken by hand or with a tool. Other blocks can only be broken with a specific tool, such as a pickaxe. Some tools allow you to break certain blocks more quickly – for example, a spade breaks sand, grass and gravel the fastest.

HEALTH POINTS AND DEATH

In Survival mode your health points decrease if you take damage and if you don't eat. If you lose all 20 health points you will find yourself back at the respawn screen. The contents of your inventory will be dropped at the site of your demise – if you're quick you can run back and pick everything up.

DAY AND NIGHT CYCLE

A complete day/night cycle lasts 20 minutes – 10 minutes of day followed by 10 minutes of night. The sun and moon rise and fall in the sky, so check their position to give you an idea of how much day or night is left.

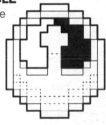

COORDINATES

Coordinates are numbers that tell you where you are. The x axis is your distance east or west from your spawn point, the z axis is your distance north or south and the y axis shows how high or low you are. Check your coordinates on desktop edition by pressing F3, or by consulting a map item in console edition.

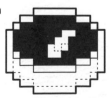

LEVELS AND EXPERIENCE

Experience points are earned through mining, defeating mobs and players, using furnaces and breeding animals. Experience orbs will appear and you'll automatically collect them if you're standing close enough. Experience points add up into levels, and you can use experience points to make enchanted tools, weapons and armour with new abilities.

THE MINECRAFT LANDSCAPE

This section is all about the physical landscape of your Minecraft world. You'll learn about the different biomes you might spawn in and discover the pros and cons of settling in each. You'll also learn where to search for fascinating naturally generated structures and valuable loot that will help you on your journey.

BIOMES

When you spawn you'll find yourself in one of several possible biomes – regions with different environments and features. There are advantages and disadvantages to settling in each biome, so you'll need to decide whether you're happy to stay put or if you'll need to search for a more hospitable area.

DESERT

Desert biomes are barren and inhospitable. Passive mobs don't spawn here, and rain doesn't fall, so finding and growing food is difficult. Visit deserts to collect resources but build your base in a more hospitable biome.

DESERT WELL

Desert wells can sometimes be found, too – these are largely decorative but can also be used as a water source.

CACTUS

There are no trees to provide wood - the surface is covered with sand, dead bushes and cacti.

Desert temples and villages are common features. Both are a great source of materials and also contain loot chests in which you can find more valuable items and blocks.

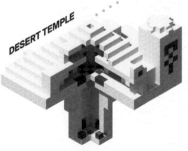
DESERT TEMPLE

DID YOU KNOW?

Look out for fossils when mining in desert biomes – they generate 15-24 blocks below the surface and are made of bone blocks. It's thought they are the remains of giant, extinct creatures ...

SAVANNA

Savannas are arid, flat biomes covered with dry grass, tall grass and acacia trees. The flat terrain is easy to build on, but farming can be more difficult due to lack of rain.

HORSE

Horses spawn frequently in savannas. See page 43 for more info on horses.

NPC VILLAGE

NPC (non-player character) villages are common, making them a good biome in which to gather resources. See page 34 for more info.

EXTREME HILLS

Extreme hills are impressive to look at, but building is difficult due to lack of flat ground, and exploring is dangerous as you can fall from the many cliffs.

EMERALD ORE

Emerald ore only generates in extreme hills, so it's a good biome for mining.

SILVERFISH

Watch out for monster eggs which contain silverfish.

MONSTER EGG

FOREST

Forests are an ideal spawn point as they provide lots of wood for crafting. The surface is covered with oak and birch trees, as well as regular grass and patches of tall grass.

WOLF

Wolves, which can be tamed to be pets, are commonly found here, but be aware that hostile mobs can use the shade under trees to stay alive during the day.

FOREST VARIANTS

Flower forests have fewer trees but an abundance of colourful flowers on the ground.

As its name suggests, the birch forest variant contains only birch trees.

BIRCH FOREST

FLOWER FOREST

MOJANG STUFF

The way each world is generated has changed a lot over the years. If you play on really old maps, strange things can happen, because the game tries to match the old environment with the new data for how biomes form. Deserts can suddenly be covered in snow, and once-flowing rivers and lakes can freeze over.

ROOFED FOREST

Roofed forest biomes are so named because of the dense covering of dark oak trees and huge mushrooms that block out most of the sunlight.

HOSTILE MOBS

Hostile mobs often spawn during the day in this gloomy biome, so it's best avoided until you're experienced and well-equipped.

HUGE MUSHROOM

Unless planted on mycelium, huge mushrooms need a light level of 12 or lower to grow. See page 83 for more info on mycelium.

JUNGLE

Jungles are difficult to travel across and build in due to the hilly terrain and dense covering of trees and bushes. Hostile mobs survive well here and can spawn in the daytime as the tree canopy blocks out a lot of sunlight. This is the only biome in which you can find melons and cocoa. Jungles are worth a visit but avoid settling in these biomes when you first spawn.

OCELOT

Ocelots spawn exclusively in jungles. See page 42 for more info.

JUNGLE TEMPLE

Jungle temples are common and contain trapped loot chests – see page 31 for more info.

ICE PLAINS

Ice plains are flat, snow-covered biomes in which all exposed water sources have frozen to ice. Sugar cane is often found here, but farming is difficult since water freezes. There aren't many trees, so it's not ideal for beginners.

TIP

Ice plains are a great biome in which to collect snow to make snow golems – utility mobs that throw snowballs at hostile mobs to knock them backwards. Stack two snow blocks vertically then place a pumpkin on top to craft. Pumpkins can be found growing on grass blocks throughout the Overworld.

POLAR BEAR

Polar bears are common in ice plains. See page 49 for more info.

SNOW GOLEMS

STRAY

Strays are skeletons that shoot slowness arrows at players.

IGLOO

Igloos generate in ice plains. See page 32 for more info.

ICE PLAINS VARIANTS

ICE PLAINS SPIKES

In this variant biome you'll find large spikes of ice. Some can reach over 50 blocks in height.

FROZEN RIVER

As its name suggests, you'll find a frozen river running through this variant biome.

PLAINS

Plains are flat and grassy, with only a sparse covering of trees. NPC villages are commonly found here. They're one of only a few biomes in which horses spawn naturally. They're relatively easy to build in so they're great for beginners and for settling long-term.

PASSIVE MOBS

Plains are a great source of food due to the abundance of passive mobs.

PLAINS VARIANT

SUNFLOWER

This rare variant of the plains biome is covered in sunflowers, all pointing east to help you get your bearings.

SWAMP

Swamps are flat and covered with small pools of water which often contain lily pads. Building on the flooded surface is difficult, but there is plenty of opportunity to fish and mushrooms are common. Many of the pools contain clay, which can be crafted into bricks.

SLIME

Swamps are the only biome in which slimes spawn at surface level. See page 63 for more info about slimes.

WITCH HUT

WITCH

Witch huts and witches are commonly found here. See page 62 for more info on witches.

You might find fossils 15-24 blocks below the surface of swamps.

OCEAN

Although not a good biome in which to live, oceans are an excellent source of fish and squid. In the deep ocean variant you'll find ocean monuments containing treasure and guardians, so they're worth a visit once you're a little more experienced.

OCEAN MONUMENT

GUARDIAN

See page 33 for more info on ocean monuments.

Guardians spawn in and around ocean monuments. See page 58 for more info.

Mycelium is a block on which mushrooms and huge mushrooms grow at any light level.

MUSHROOM ISLAND

The rare mushroom island biome can be found in the middle of the ocean. It's a mixture of hills and plains, covered in mycelium. Mushroom island biomes are one of only two biomes in which huge mushrooms grow naturally. The biome is a safe refuge for beginners, but trees don't grow here so you'll need to move elsewhere if you want to craft anything useful.

MOOSHROOM

Mooshrooms are the only mob that spawns here – there are no hostile mobs.

MESA

Mesa biomes are rare. Largely composed of hardened clay and red sand, trees are uncommon and there are no passive mobs to provide meat, so avoid this biome when you first spawn. Gold ore generates at all levels here.

MESA VARIANTS

ABANDONED MINESHAFT

MESA PLATEAU

These variants contain clay spikes and flat, tree-covered areas respectively.

Abandoned mineshafts generate at surface level so mesas are a great mining spot.

MESA (BRYCE)

TAIGA

Taiga biomes are a great source of wood due to the abundance of spruce trees, making them a great starting point for beginners.

TAIGA VARIANT

MEGA TAIGA

RABBIT

Wolves and rabbits are commonly found here, but there isn't much else so you'll want to move on once you've set yourself up with the basics.

THE NETHER

You'll never spawn here, but more advanced players will want to visit the Nether – a hellish dimension filled with new and terrifying hostile mobs. The Nether is a great source of unique materials such as glowstone, which can be used as a light source, and Nether quartz, which can be turned into quartz for building.

NETHER PORTAL

The Nether is accessed via a portal that you'll build from obsidian then set alight to activate.

HOSTILE MOBS

Nether mobs drop an array of useful items, many of which are needed for potions.

NETHER FORTRESS

Nether fortresses are the only naturally generated structure in the Nether. They contain several useful materials including Nether wart which you'll need for potions.

MOJANG STUFF

There's no water allowed in the Nether. Or is there? Though water poured from a bucket instantly evaporates, clever players have found ways to smuggle water down there – transporting it as ice, for instance. All of these workarounds have now been countered. Or so it's thought ...

THE END

The End is composed of several islands floating in the Void. Only the most advanced players dare venture there ...

ENDER DRAGON

MAIN ISLAND

The main island is accessed via an End portal in a stronghold in the Overworld – see page 35 for more info. If you want to get out of there alive and visit the outer islands you'll need to defeat the ultimate boss mob – the ender dragon.

OUTER ISLANDS

For those skilful enough to defeat the dragon, you must then find a way to the outer islands. There you'll find unique blocks, as well as rare items such as elytra (wings that allow you to glide), a decorative dragon head and a new hostile mob – the shulker.

MOJANG STUFF

As in the Nether, sleeping in a bed in the End will cause it to explode. One speedrun challenge in hardcore mode is to find a way of placing beds during the climactic battle so that you are partly shielded from the explosion, but inflict maximum damage to the dragon as it swoops in. Timing is everything!

NATURALLY GENERATED STRUCTURES

If you know where to look you'll find naturally generated structures all around you. These structures contain valuable materials and sometimes loot chests, too, but they're dangerous and often contain traps. Proceed with caution.

ABANDONED MINESHAFT

Usually found underground, abandoned mineshafts are an excellent place to mine for ores.

Beware of cave spider spawners which are surrounded by a heavy layer of cobwebs. Cave spiders are venomous and can soon overpower you in the narrow corridors.

CAVE SPIDER

Watch out for lava streams and pools, which are common underground.

FOUND:

ANY BIOME

Look out for minecarts in corridors – these contain loot chests.

MINECART WITH CHEST

DESERT TEMPLE

Desert temples are found in desert biomes. They are constructed from various sandstone blocks, with decorative blocks of orange and blue hardened clay. You can mine these blocks for use in your own constructions.

Desert temples may be partially buried in sand and can be difficult to spot. Look out for sandstone and orange hardened clay, or a tower protruding from the landscape.

You'll find a hidden chamber directly below the blue and orange hardened clay in the centre of the main chamber floor. This hidden chamber contains four loot chests.

LOOT CHEST

The pressure plate in the centre of the chests is rigged to a TNT block and will detonate if you step or fall directly onto it. Descend carefully.

TNT

FOUND:

DESERT

DUNGEON

Dungeons are small rooms built out of moss stone and cobblestone. They usually generate underground, and you can wander into them fairly easily. Keep an eye out for moss stone or flames flickering in the darkness when mining.

You'll find a zombie, skeleton or spider spawner in the centre of the dungeon, which you can disable by placing torches around and on top of it. Alternatively, you could use the spawner for combat practice.

Each dungeon contains up to two loot chests which can be raided once you've dealt with the spawner.

You can easily find yourself swarmed by hostile mobs in such a small, enclosed space. Get your back up against a wall if you're struggling.

FOUND:

ANY BIOME

MONSTER SPAWNER

JUNGLE TEMPLE

Built from cobblestone, moss stone and chiselled stone bricks, mysterious jungle temples have three floors and can be accessed via an entrance at ground level.

Down in the basement you'll find three levers. When pulled in the right order they'll reveal a secret chamber back on the ground floor which contains a loot chest.

The top floor is empty but can be mined for moss stone.

MOSS STONE

Once you've collected the loot you can mine the trap mechanisms and redstone for your own use.

FOUND:

JUNGLE

Further along the corridor from the levers you'll find two dispensers filled with arrows. Find a way to pass without walking through the tripwire and you'll be rewarded with another loot chest at the end of the corridor.

IGLOO

Igloos are small structures composed of snow blocks. They make useful emergency shelters.

Inside you'll find carpet, a bed, a crafting table and a furnace.

Half of igloos also contain a basement, accessed via a trapdoor under the carpet.

The basement contains a brewing stand, a loot chest, a cauldron and two cells imprisoning a villager priest and a zombie villager priest. Mine the brewing stand and cauldron with a pickaxe – you'll need them to brew potions.

FOUND:

ICE PLAINS/COLD TAIGA

Watch out for silverfish in the basement – some of the wall blocks are actually monster eggs.

OCEAN MONUMENT

Ocean monuments are grand underwater structures built from a variety of prismarine blocks and lit by sea lanterns.

Ocean monuments are protected by guardians and elder guardians – see page 58-59 to learn more about these creatures.

GUARDIAN

ELDER GUARDIAN

The layout is different for each monument, but they always contain at least 6 chambers.

Head to the centre and you'll find the treasure chamber. This contains 8 gold blocks encased in dark prismarine.

FOUND:

DEEP OCEAN

Wet sponge can sometimes be found hanging from the ceiling of one of the chambers. Dry it in a furnace and it can be used to remove water blocks through absorption.

NPC VILLAGE

Home to your friendly local villagers, NPC villages contain a variety of structures with different functions, from houses and farms to blacksmiths and libraries.

Watch out for zombie villagers, especially in small villages with no iron golem.

ZOMBIE VILLAGER

Villagers spawn in the building relating to their profession. During the day they leave their buildings and wander around the village.

VILLAGER

The blacksmiths contain a loot chest. Among other things you might find saddles, armour, diamonds and obsidian inside.

Iron golems spawn in villages with 10 or more villagers and 21 or more doors. These utility mobs exist to protect the helpless villagers from hostile mobs.

FOUND:

PLAINS / SAVANNA / TAIGA / DESERT

Farms can be raided for crops, which can be eaten or used to start a new farm back at your base.

STRONGHOLD

Strongholds are found underground, and sometimes underwater. You'll need to find a stronghold if you want to visit the End.

Throw eyes of ender to locate your nearest stronghold. Each eye will travel a short distance in the right direction. When they stop travelling and fall onto the same spot, dig down to find the stronghold.

Strongholds vary in size. They are composed of several rooms, connected by a maze of corridors and staircases. It's easy to get lost in large strongholds as you search for the End portal room.

Look out for loot chests as you explore. These may contain everything from enchanted books to diamond horse armour.

FOUND:

ANY BIOME

The End portal room contains an incomplete End portal and a silverfish spawner. You'll need to fill the remaining End portal frames with eyes of ender to activate it, then jump through to be transported to the End.

WOODLAND MANSION

Woodland mansions are a rare sight in roofed forest biomes. Built from wood and cobblestone, they have several floors, many rooms and offer an abundance of useful resources. Sound too good to be true? Unfortunately they're also home to some of Minecraft's most dangerous mobs.

In addition to the usual hostile mobs, vindicator, evoker and vex mobs spawn inside the mansion. These boss-like mobs are highly dangerous and only skilled players should attempt to take them on. See pages 64-65 to learn more.

VEX

VINDICATOR

EVOKER

You may find several farming areas on the ground floor, including a tree farm, mushroom farm and pumpkin and melon patches.

FOUND:

ROOFED FOREST

Several rooms have a more
homely feel – dining rooms
contain tables, flower pots and
bookshelves, and you might find
many bedrooms, too.

Among the more sinister
structures you might find are altar-
style constructs, strange platforms
and prison cells. There might also
be a map room, which suggests
the vindicators and evokers are
plotting something.

2

MOBS

You're not alone in this mysterious new world. In this section you'll discover the differences between passive, neutral and hostile mobs. You'll learn where to find them, how to defend yourself from neutral and hostile mob attacks and, most importantly, what each mob drops when defeated.

PASSIVE MOBS

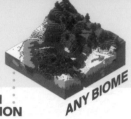

As you explore the Overworld you'll come across a variety of passive mobs which can easily be defeated with a tool or weapon. Most drop useful items, including meat which will be cooked if they are killed when on fire.

SPAWN
LOCATION

ANY BIOME

CHICKEN

BEHAVIOUR
Chickens spawn in grassy areas. They wander around, clucking and laying eggs every 5-10 minutes.

SPECIAL SKILLS
When falling, chickens slow their descent by flapping their wings so they don't take damage.

DROPS WHEN DEFEATED

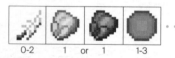

0-2	1	or	1	1-3

DROPS WHEN ALIVE

∞

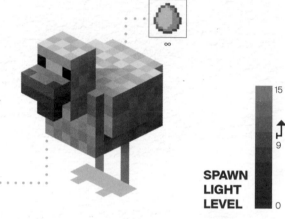

15

9

SPAWN
LIGHT
LEVEL

0

BAT

BEHAVIOUR
Bats spawn in caves across the Overworld. They hang upside-down when idle, but otherwise can be seen flying around erratically.

SPECIAL SKILLS
Bats are the only passive mob that spawns in the dark and that can fly.

DROPS WHEN DEFEATED

0

MOJANG STUFF

The high-pitched squeak the bat makes was toned down several times after players said it hurt their ears.

15

3

SPAWN
LIGHT
LEVEL

0

PIG

BEHAVIOUR

Pigs roam the Overworld in groups of 3-4, oinking randomly. They will follow any player that is within 5 blocks of them and is holding a carrot, a carrot on a stick, a potato or beetroot.

See page 75 for a fishing rod recipe. Carrots can be found in NPC village farms and can be dropped by zombies.

CARROT ON A STICK RECIPE

SPECIAL SKILLS

Pigs can be ridden, although they aren't very fast. You'll need to saddle them first, then lead them around using a carrot on a stick. They will eat the carrot over time so you'll need to keep an eye on its durability bar. Saddles can be found in naturally generated chests. A saddled pig will drop its saddle upon death.

DROPS WHEN DEFEATED

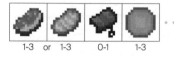

| 1-3 | or | 1-3 | 0-1 | 1-3 |

SPAWN LIGHT LEVEL

15

9

0

SHEEP

BEHAVIOUR

Sheep wander around, bleating occasionally and eating grass blocks.

SPECIAL SKILLS

Sheep drop 1 wool when they die, but 1-3 wool if you shear them while they're alive. The wool will grow back after shearing. You can also dye a sheep before you shear it to permanently change the wool's colour. Dyes can be crafted from flowers, lapis lazuli, cocoa beans and ink sacs.

DROPS WHEN ALIVE

1-3

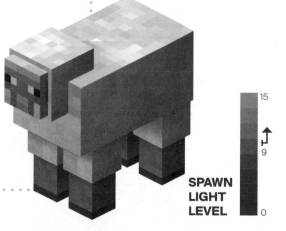

DROPS WHEN DEFEATED

| 1 | 1-2 | or | 1-2 | 1-3 |

SPAWN LIGHT LEVEL

15

9

0

OCELOT

BEHAVIOUR
Ocelots creep through jungles, occasionally attacking chickens. They avoid players and hostile mobs.

SPECIAL SKILLS
Ocelots are immune to fall damage. They can be tamed into cats by feeding them raw fish. Stand within 10 blocks of an ocelot, then wait for it to enter begging mode – it will walk right up to you and look at you. Don't make any sudden movements or you'll scare it off. Feed it fish and it may turn into a tabby, tuxedo or Siamese cat. Tamed cats will follow you around and will no longer attack chickens. Ocelots and tamed cats both scare creepers away.

SPAWN LOCATION

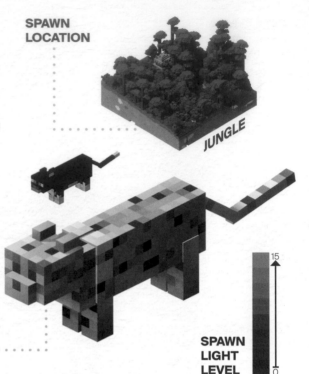

JUNGLE

DROPS WHEN DEFEATED

1-3

SPAWN LIGHT LEVEL

15

0

RABBIT

BEHAVIOUR
Rabbits hop around, avoiding players, hostile mobs and wolves. They seek out and eat mature carrot crops.

SPECIAL SKILLS
Rabbits will approach you if you're within 8 blocks and are holding carrots or dandelions. They will go over cliffs to reach carrots, but not through lava.

DROPS WHEN DEFEATED

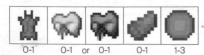

0-1   0-1 or 0-1   0-1   1-3

SPAWN LIGHT LEVEL

15

0

SQUID

BEHAVIOUR

Squid move through water using their tentacles. If attacked, they try to swim away. They suffocate if not in water.

SPECIAL SKILLS

Squid can swim against a current. They also have an impressive set of teeth, although they are harmless.

DROPS WHEN DEFEATED

1-3	1-3

SPAWN LOCATION

ANY BIOME
(IN WATER)

15

SPAWN LIGHT LEVEL

0

HORSE

BEHAVIOUR

Horses roam in herds of 2-6. They can have one of 35 different colour and marking combinations. Donkeys are a smaller variant of horse. If a horse breeds with a donkey they will produce a mule.

SPECIAL SKILLS

Horses are one of the fastest methods of transport, but they need to be tamed first. Tame a horse by mounting it repeatedly until it stops throwing you off, then saddle it so it can be ridden. Saddles can be found in naturally generated chests. Donkeys and mules can also be equipped with chests and used to transport items. When killed, horses will drop any equipment they have, and donkeys and mules will drop their chest, if equipped, plus its contents.

DROPS WHEN DEFEATED

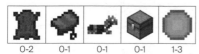

0-2	0-1	0-1	0-1	1-3

SPAWN LOCATION

SAVANNAS/
PLAINS

15

SPAWN LIGHT LEVEL

0

COW

BEHAVIOUR

Cows travel in groups and can be heard mooing from quite some distance.

SPECIAL SKILLS

Cows can be milked by using a bucket on them. See page 73 for a bucket recipe. They also follow you if you're holding wheat within 10 blocks of them. They may drop leather when they die, which can be used in several crafting recipes, and will drop meat which will be cooked if they were killed by fire.

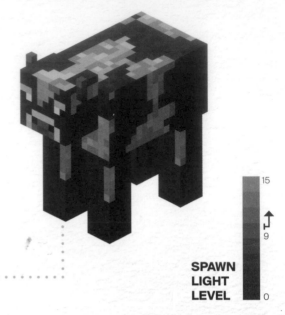

DROPS WHEN DEFEATED

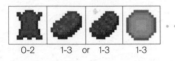

0-2	1-3 or	1-3	1-3

SPAWN
LIGHT
LEVEL

15

9

0

MOOSHROOM

BEHAVIOUR

Mooshrooms can only be found in mushroom biomes. They wander around in herds of 4-8, avoiding danger such as cliffs and lava.

SPAWN LOCATION

MUSHROOM ISLAND BIOME

SPECIAL SKILLS

Mooshrooms can be milked by using a bucket on them. They can also be milked with a bowl to produce mushroom stew, and sheared for 5 red mushrooms which will turn them into regular cows. In all other respects they are very similar to cows – they may drop leather upon death, and will drop 1-3 pieces of meat, which will be cooked if they were killed by fire.

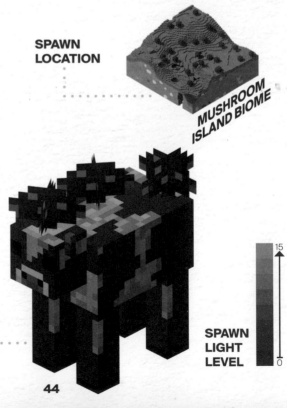

DROPS WHEN DEFEATED

0-2	1-3 or	1-3	1-3

SPAWN
LIGHT
LEVEL

15

0

LLAMA

BEHAVIOUR

Llamas like to stay together in herds. If one llama is led by a player, nearby llamas will follow, forming a caravan. They are hostile towards wolves and will spit at them, dealing a small amount of damage. They will also spit at any player who attacks them.

SPECIAL SKILLS

Llamas can be ridden. You'll need to tame them first by riding them a few times, with an empty hand, until they stop throwing you off. Once tame you can equip a llama with a chest. You can also equip llamas with carpets to change the appearance of their saddle.

DROPS WHEN DEFEATED

| 0-2 | 0-1 | 0-1 | 1-3 |

SPAWN
LOCATIONS

SAVANNA

EXTREME HILLS

DID YOU KNOW?

Each llama has its own unique strength rating which determines how many items it can carry. They're all equally adorable, however.

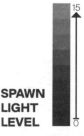

15

**SPAWN
LIGHT
LEVEL**

0

VILLAGER

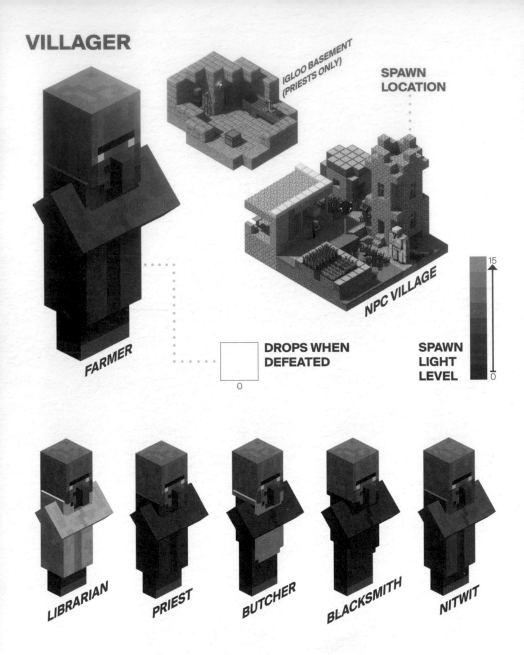

IGLOO BASEMENT
(PRIESTS ONLY)

SPAWN
LOCATION

NPC VILLAGE

FARMER

DROPS WHEN
DEFEATED

0

SPAWN
LIGHT
LEVEL

15

0

LIBRARIAN   PRIEST   BUTCHER   BLACKSMITH   NITWIT

VARIANTS

Villagers are human figures with one of five different professions: farmer, librarian, priest, blacksmith or butcher. The sixth villager has no profession and is known as the nitwit villager. Within each profession are several careers – for example, farmers can be fishermen, shepherds or fletchers.

BEHAVIOUR

Villagers wander around the village during the day, socialising. They have been known to share their food with any villagers who don't have enough. They will head into the buildings at night or if it rains, and flee from zombies, which can turn them into zombie villagers.

SPECIAL SKILLS

Villagers will breed, creating baby villagers, until the number of adult villagers is greater than 35% of the number of doors in the village. Each villager has 8 secret inventory slots and will collect any carrots, potatoes, wheat, seeds, beetroot, beetroot seeds and bread they find.

VILLAGER TRADING

With the exception of the nitwit, all adult villagers like to trade goods for emeralds. Interact with a villager and a menu will appear, displaying an offer. Place the item they are requesting in the left-hand slot, and the item they are offering will appear on the right for you to take.

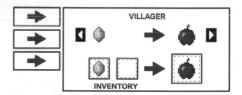

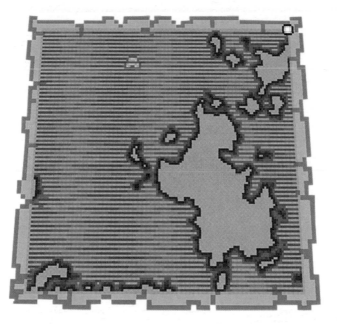

Some librarians, known as cartographers, will trade exploration maps for emeralds and a compass. These maps are very useful for tracking down loot since they can be used to locate woodland mansions and ocean monuments.

NEUTRAL MOBS

Unfortunately, not all mobs are passive sources of food. A handful of mobs are classified as neutral, which means their behaviour varies and they can become hostile under certain circumstances. Keep an eye out for them – they drop some useful items that will aid your progress in different ways.

WOLF

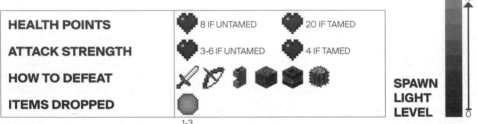

HEALTH POINTS	8 IF UNTAMED	20 IF TAMED
ATTACK STRENGTH	3-6 IF UNTAMED	4 IF TAMED
HOW TO DEFEAT		
ITEMS DROPPED	1-3	

SPAWN LIGHT LEVEL

15

0

BEHAVIOUR
Wolves roam in packs of 4 and will attack rabbits, skeletons and sheep on sight. A wolf will become hostile towards any player or mob that attacks them, and any nearby wolves will become hostile, too. Hostile wolves have red eyes and growl.

SPAWN LOCATIONS

TAIGA

FOREST

SPECIAL SKILLS
Wolves can be tamed by feeding them bones. Once tame they will wear a red collar and follow you around. Tamed wolves can teleport to their owner and will attack any mob that you attack, with the exception of creepers.

ATTACK METHOD
A hostile wolf will pounce on you, inflicting damage with each hit.

POLAR BEAR

HEALTH POINTS	30
ATTACK STRENGTH	4-9
HOW TO DEFEAT	
ITEMS DROPPED	0-2 0-2 1-3

SPAWN
LIGHT
LEVEL

BEHAVIOUR

Adult polar bears are neutral but will become hostile if attacked by a player or if they have cubs and a player gets too close. Cubs are passive and will run away if attacked, but all the adults within a 41 x 41 x 41 area will become hostile and attack you in retaliation.

SPECIAL SKILLS

Polar bears are fast swimmers. They may drop fish when defeated.

SPAWN LOCATIONS

ICE MOUNTAINS

ICE SPIKES

ICE PLAINS

ATTACK METHOD

Polar bears will rear up onto their back legs and strike you from above with their front paws.

MOJANG STUFF

Jeb, lead developer for Minecraft, added polar bears to the game because his wife likes them.

49

SPIDER

HEALTH POINTS	❤ 16
ATTACK STRENGTH	❤ 2-3
HOW TO DEFEAT	
ITEMS DROPPED	0-2 0-1 5

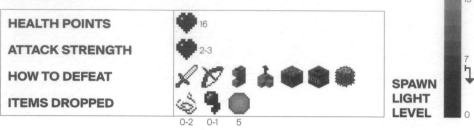

SPAWN LIGHT LEVEL

15
7
0

BEHAVIOUR

Spiders are hostile to players and iron golems if the light level is 11 or lower. If the light level is higher, they won't attack unless provoked. Once hostile they will continue to pursue you, even if the light level increases.

SPECIAL SKILLS

Spiders can climb over obstacles and up walls. They are immune to poison.

ATTACK METHOD

Spiders will pounce on their opponent, inflicting damage with each hit.

SPAWN LOCATIONS

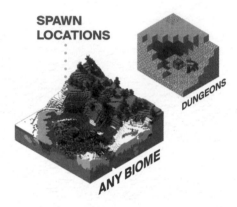

DUNGEONS

ANY BIOME

VARIANT: CAVE SPIDER

SPECIAL SKILLS

Cave spiders inflict venom, poisoning you over time. They can fit through spaces that are 1 block wide and half a block tall.

HOW TO DEFEAT	

SPAWN LOCATION

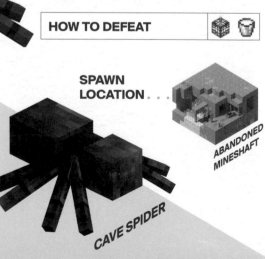

ABANDONED MINESHAFT

CAVE SPIDER

DID YOU KNOW? ↗

Occasionally a regular spider spawns with a skeleton rider. These horrifying spider jockeys have the speed and agility of a spider combined with the archery skills of a skeleton, making them truly formidable.

ENDERMAN

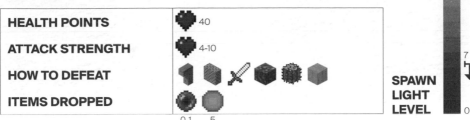

HEALTH POINTS	40
ATTACK STRENGTH	4-10
HOW TO DEFEAT	
ITEMS DROPPED	0-1 5

SPAWN LIGHT LEVEL

15

7

0

BEHAVIOUR

Endermen are not hostile towards players unless provoked by attack or by a player looking directly at their head. Once provoked they will shake and scream, then launch themselves at you to attack. Endermen will also attack endermites on sight.

SPAWN LOCATIONS

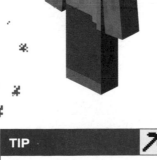

OVERWORLD

THE NETHER

THE END

SPECIAL SKILLS

Endermen teleport to avoid danger. They drop ender pearls which, when thrown, will teleport you. They can also pick up and place certain blocks.

ATTACK METHOD

Endermen will teleport to you and hit you, inflicting damage.

MOJANG STUFF

Endermen hate endermites, so you can use the nasty little bugs as a handy distraction. You can, for instance, put an endermite into a minecart and set it rolling past endermen, using it to lure them away, or, if you are particularly well-prepared, into a pit.

TIP

Wear a pumpkin on your head and an enderman will remain neutral even if you look at it. See page 89 to discover how to equip armour.

HOSTILE MOBS

Hostile mobs can make your life incredibly difficult and can easily send you back to the respawn screen. They can be particularly dangerous if you encounter them in a small space or whilst mining underground, but, like neutral mobs, they drop some useful items if you manage to defeat them.

ZOMBIE

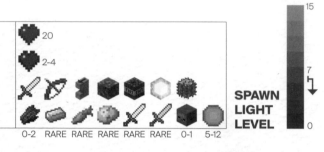

HEALTH POINTS	♥ 20	
ATTACK STRENGTH	♥ 2-4	
HOW TO DEFEAT		
ITEMS DROPPED		

0-2 RARE RARE RARE RARE RARE 0-1 5-12

15

7

0

SPAWN LIGHT LEVEL

SPAWN LOCATION

ANY BIOME

BEHAVIOUR

Zombies spawn in groups of 4, at light levels of 7 or less. Some zombies spawn wearing armour, which they may then drop upon death. They can't spawn on transparent blocks like glass. They shamble around slowly, with their arms outstretched, making a moaning noise. They catch fire in the sun, so will try to seek shade when the sun rises in the morning.

DID YOU KNOW?

Unlike naturally spawned equipment, zombies never fail to drop the equipment that they have picked up when defeated. Evidence of a guilty conscience, perhaps ...

SPECIAL SKILLS

Zombies can break through wooden doors if your difficulty level is set to hard. They can pick up items from the ground, including weapons and tools which they will use, and armour which they will put on. When wearing helmets, zombies are safe from burning in the sun.

USEFUL DROPS

Zombies drop 0-2 pieces of rotten flesh, which you can eat in an emergency but you might get food poisoning as a result. You can also use rotten flesh to breed and heal tamed wolves. Zombies also drop any equipment they have picked up, such as weapons, tools and armour, and will drop their head if killed by a charged creeper's explosion.

ATTACK METHOD

Zombies will pursue players, villagers and iron golems on sight, from 40 blocks away. They aren't a big threat unless you encounter a large group of them – they'll bump into you, inflicting damage and knocking you backwards with each hit, potentially into lava or over a cliff.

ZOMBIE VARIANTS

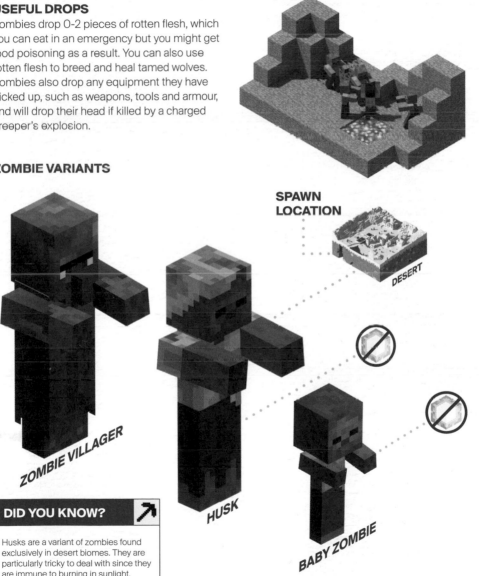

SPAWN LOCATION

DESERT

ZOMBIE VILLAGER

HUSK

BABY ZOMBIE

DID YOU KNOW?

Husks are a variant of zombies found exclusively in desert biomes. They are particularly tricky to deal with since they are immune to burning in sunlight.

CREEPER

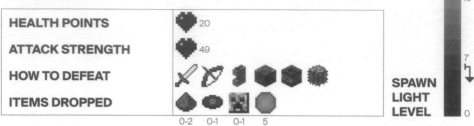

HEALTH POINTS	20			
ATTACK STRENGTH	49			
HOW TO DEFEAT				
ITEMS DROPPED				

0-2   0-1   0-1   5

SPAWN
LIGHT
LEVEL

15

7

0

BEHAVIOUR

Creepers move around almost silently, searching for players to target. They have a TNT core that detonates when they are close enough to a player.

SPAWN LOCATION

ANY BIOME

SPECIAL SKILLS

Creepers are immune to burning in sunlight, and continue to creep around in search of players after the sun has risen. They also have the ability to climb up ladders and vines and can do so when pursuing their targets.

ATTACK METHOD

When they're within 3 blocks of a player, creepers will hiss and flash before exploding. Once they begin to hiss you have 1.5 seconds to get out of the blast radius (7 blocks) if you want to stop the explosion.

USEFUL DROPS

Creepers drop gunpowder, needed to craft TNT, and will drop a music disc if killed by a skeleton's arrow. You'll need a jukebox to play a music disc. Jukeboxes can be crafted from any wood planks.

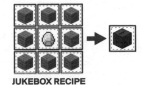

TNT RECIPE

JUKEBOX RECIPE

VARIANT: CHARGED CREEPER

SPAWN LOCATION

When lightning strikes within 3-4 blocks of a regular creeper.

LIGHTNING

ANY BIOME

SPECIAL SKILLS

The charged creeper's explosion is twice as powerful as that of a regular creeper. This explosion will cause any zombies, skeletons or regular creepers unfortunate enough to be in the vicinity to drop their mob heads. These rare blocks can be used for decoration or worn instead of a helmet. Wearing a mob head will reduce the chance of that mob recognising you as a player and attacking.

SKELETON

HEALTH POINTS	 20
ATTACK STRENGTH	1-5
HOW TO DEFEAT	
ITEMS DROPPED	

0-2   0-2   RARE   RARE   5-9

SPAWN LIGHT LEVEL

15

7

0

BEHAVIOUR

Skeletons rattle as they move around, searching for players to attack. They seek out shade at sunrise to avoid burning.

ATTACK METHOD

Skeletons will pursue you on sight. Once they're within 8 blocks they'll shoot you with arrows, circling you at the same time to make it difficult for you to hit them.

SPAWN LOCATIONS

NETHER FORTRESSES

ANY BIOME

DUNGEONS

SPECIAL SKILLS AND USEFUL DROPS

Skeletons can climb ladders. They can pick up items, including tools, weapons and armour, which they will equip/use. They may also spawn wearing armour. Upon death they will drop anything they have picked up, and may drop any naturally spawned equipment.

VARIANT: STRAY

Strays only appear in snowy biomes. They shoot tipped arrows that inflict slowness for 30 seconds. They may also drop 1 tipped arrow upon death.

SPAWN LOCATIONS

ICE SPIKES   ICE MOUNTAINS

ICE PLAINS

SKELETON HORSEMAN

HEALTH POINTS	❤ 35		
ATTACK STRENGTH	❤ 1-10		
HOW TO DEFEAT	🏹		
ITEMS DROPPED	🦴 🏹 ⬤		
	0-2 0-2 5		

SPAWN LIGHT LEVEL

15
7
0

BEHAVIOUR

Skeleton horsemen move very fast, and circle their opponent in the same way a skeleton does. If you kill a skeleton horseman, the horse will become tame and you can saddle and ride it.

LIGHTNING

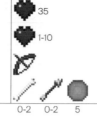

SPAWN LOCATION

A skeleton trap horse spawns when a regular horse is struck by lightning. When a player comes within 10 blocks of a skeleton trap horse and lightning strikes the horse again, it will transform into four skeleton horsemen.

ANY BIOME

SPECIAL SKILLS

Skeleton horsemen spawn with enchanted bows and helmets.

ATTACK METHOD

Skeleton riders attack on sight, shooting players with their bows.

GUARDIAN

HEALTH POINTS	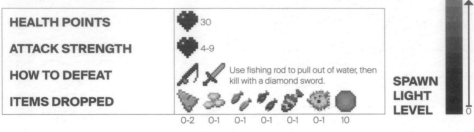 30	
ATTACK STRENGTH	4-9	
HOW TO DEFEAT		Use fishing rod to pull out of water, then kill with a diamond sword.
ITEMS DROPPED		
	0-2 0-1 0-1 0-1 0-1 0-1 10	

BEHAVIOUR

Guardians exist to protect the treasure in ocean monuments. They patrol the monuments, attacking players and squid on sight.

ATTACK METHOD

Guardians will shoot you with their laser, which can reach you from up to 15 blocks away. They also extend their defensive spikes, and if you hit them whilst they are extended you will take 2 damage points (1 heart).

SPECIAL SKILLS

Despite living in water, guardians do not suffocate on dry land, although they squeak angrily and flop around.

SPAWN LOCATION

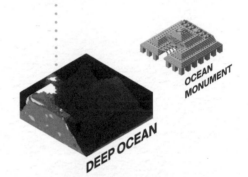

OCEAN MONUMENT

DEEP OCEAN

DID YOU KNOW?

It won't have escaped your notice that ocean monuments are found underwater. So, if you want to visit one, you'll need to enchant your equipment with depth strider and respiration.

ELDER GUARDIAN

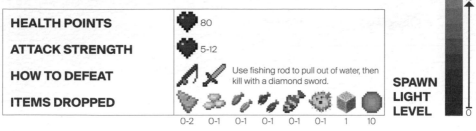

HEALTH POINTS	80	
ATTACK STRENGTH	5-12	
HOW TO DEFEAT		Use fishing rod to pull out of water, then kill with a diamond sword.
ITEMS DROPPED		

0-2 0-1 0-1 0-1 0-1 0-1 1 10

SPAWN LIGHT LEVEL

15

0

BEHAVIOUR
You'll find three elder guardians in each ocean monument – one in the top room and one in each wing – guarding the monument's treasure. They will attack players and squid on sight.

SPECIAL SKILLS
Like guardians, elder guardians do not suffocate on dry land.

ATTACK METHOD
Elder guardians have the same laser attack and defensive spikes as guardians, but can also inflict mining fatigue III for 5 minutes – blocks you mine will break more slowly and your attack speed is reduced.

SPAWN LOCATION

OCEAN MONUMENT

DEEP OCEAN

MOJANG STUFF

If elder guardians didn't cast mining fatigue III on you, breaking into ocean monuments would be too easy. But from the developers' perspective, it was quite hard to communicate what was happening. The solution – the sudden appearance on-screen of a ghostly guardian's face – ended up being one of the most successful (if unintentional) jump scares in the game.

SILVERFISH

HEALTH POINTS	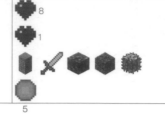	8
ATTACK STRENGTH		1
HOW TO DEFEAT		
ITEMS DROPPED		
	5	

**SPAWN
LIGHT
LEVEL**

15

11

0

BEHAVIOUR

When not spawning directly from monster spawners in strongholds, idle silverfish live in monster egg blocks and emerge when a player mines the block.

SPECIAL SKILLS

Silverfish can call other silverfish to their aid when they are being attacked. They can see you through walls and will use this ability to find a path to you.

ATTACK METHOD

Silverfish run towards you and inflict damage, knocking you backwards upon contact. You can easily find yourself swarmed.

SPAWN LOCATIONS

Silverfish spawn when monster egg blocks are broken in strongholds, igloo basements and in extreme hills biomes. They also appear from monster spawners in strongholds.

EXTREME HILLS

STRONGHOLD

IGLOO BASEMENT

DID YOU KNOW?

If you're quick and defeat a silverfish in a single hit with a diamond sword, nearby silverfish won't be alerted.

ENDERMITE

HEALTH POINTS	8		
ATTACK STRENGTH	2-3		
HOW TO DEFEAT			
ITEMS DROPPED	3		

SPAWN
LIGHT
LEVEL

15

7

0

BEHAVIOUR

Endermites are the smallest mob. They occasionally spawn when an ender pearl is thrown. They scuttle about, leaving a trail of purple particles behind them, and attack players within 16 blocks. When not attacking players they sometimes try to burrow into blocks.

SPECIAL SKILLS

Endermites will despawn after two minutes. If one endermite is attacked, all nearby endermites will retaliate.

ATTACK METHOD

Endermites run towards you and inflict damage by bumping into you. As with silverfish, you can easily find yourself swarmed.

SPAWN LOCATIONS

Endermites occasionally spawn when an ender pearl is thrown.

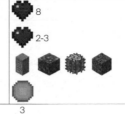

THE END

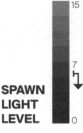

THE NETHER

OVERWORLD

WITCH

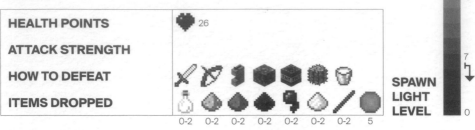

HEALTH POINTS	❤ 26							
ATTACK STRENGTH								
HOW TO DEFEAT								
ITEMS DROPPED								
	0-2	0-2	0-2	0-2	0-2	0-2	0-2	5

SPAWN LIGHT LEVEL

15
7
0

BEHAVIOUR
Witches wander around, searching for players. Their cackle will alert you to their presence.

USEFUL DROPS
Witches may drop a maximum of 2 of up to 3 of the items listed under ITEMS DROPPED; they can drop a maximum of 6 items in total.

ATTACK METHOD
Witches throw harmful splash potions (poison, slowness, weakness and harming) at you, whilst drinking helpful potions to heal themselves.

SPAWN LOCATIONS
Witches can also spawn when lightning strikes within 3-4 blocks of a villager.

ANY BIOME

LIGHTNING

WITCH HUT

DID YOU KNOW?
Witches aren't great at multitasking – they can't attack and drink helpful potions at the same time. Get some hits in when you see them start to heal themselves.

MOJANG STUFF
For a long time, witches had no sound effects. When they were finally implemented, the developers forgot to tell anyone. Players creeping through caves suddenly heard unfamiliar and alarming sounds emanating from the dark. Some were convinced the game was haunted!

SLIME

HEALTH POINTS	1-16
ATTACK STRENGTH	0-4
HOW TO DEFEAT	
ITEMS DROPPED	0-2 1-4

SPAWN LIGHT LEVEL

15

8

0

BEHAVIOUR

Slimes come in three sizes: big, small and tiny. They bounce around searching for players to attack and are also hostile towards iron golems.

SPECIAL SKILLS

Slimes can swim in water. They also have the ability to duplicate – if you defeat a big slime, it will split into small slimes, and if you defeat a small slime it will split into tiny slimes. Big and small slimes only drop experience points, but tiny slimes drop slimeballs which can be used in a number of crafting recipes including sticky pistons and leads.

SPAWN LOCATIONS

Slimes spawn in any biome in the Overworld, below level 40. In swamp biomes, between layers 50 and 70.

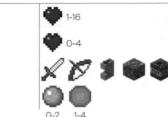

SWAMP

ANY BIOME

ATTACK METHOD

Slimes will bounce into you, inflicting damage when they make contact.

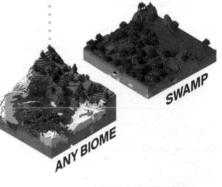

ILLAGER

Illagers are a hostile variant of regular villagers. They look similar to villagers but are dressed in dark robes and their skin has an unhealthy grey hue. There are two variants – the vindicator and the evoker – and they can be found in woodland mansions.

SPAWN LOCATION

ROOFED FOREST

WOODLAND MANSIONS

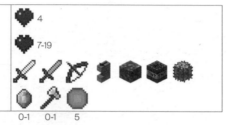

SPAWN LIGHT LEVEL

15

0

VARIANT: VINDICATOR

HEALTH POINTS	♥ 4
ATTACK STRENGTH	♥ 7-19
HOW TO DEFEAT	⚔ ⚔ 🏹 🟫 ⬛ ⬛ ⚙
ITEMS DROPPED	🔵 🔨 🟤

0-1   0-1   5

BEHAVIOUR
Vindicators spawn in groups of 2-3 inside woodland mansions in roofed forest biomes. They are hostile towards players and regular villagers and will pursue them on sight.

ATTACK METHOD
Vindicators will move quickly towards their target, brandishing their axe as a weapon then using it to deal damage.

USEFUL DROPS
Vindicators may drop emeralds when defeated which can be used to trade with their passive cousins in NPC villages.

MOJANG STUFF

The illagers were once called illvillagers and evillagers, but just dropping the 'v' was more fun.

VARIANT: EVOKER

HEALTH POINTS	♥ 24
ATTACK STRENGTH	♥ 6
HOW TO DEFEAT	⚔ ⚔ 🏹 🧨 ⬛ ⬛ ⬛
ITEMS DROPPED	🔘 ⚡ 🔘
	0-1 1 10

BEHAVIOUR
Evokers spawn alone in woodland mansions and are hostile towards players and regular villagers.

USEFUL DROPS
When defeated, evokers drop a rare and powerful item – the totem of undying. When held, this object will prevent the owner from dying.

ATTACK METHOD
The evoker has a special fang attack – it summons a stream of sharp teeth which rise up out of the floor and bite the evoker's opponent. Evokers can also summon three vexes which will join the fight.

VEX

HEALTH POINTS	♥ 14
ATTACK STRENGTH	♥ 5-13
HOW TO KILL	⚔ ⚔ 🏹 ⬛ ⬛
ITEMS DROPPED	🔘
	3

BEHAVIOUR
Vexes are summoned by evokers. Armed with swords, they fly at the nearest player or regular villager and attack.

SPECIAL SKILLS
Vexes have the ability to fly through solid blocks and can often be seen disappearing through the floor of the mansion.

ATTACK METHOD
Vexes fly at players or villagers and hit them with their sword.

3

SURVIVAL

Now that you're familiar with the Minecraft landscape and its mobs, it's time to start your first game. In this section you'll learn how to find food and materials to keep yourself safe. You'll discover how to build a shelter and a farm, how to mine for materials and how to defend yourself in combat as you explore.

YOUR FIRST DAY

When you first spawn it's a race against time to gather resources before night falls and the hostile mobs come looking for you. Every adventure is different but this step-by-step guide is one option that will keep you safe until day two.

FIRST DAY

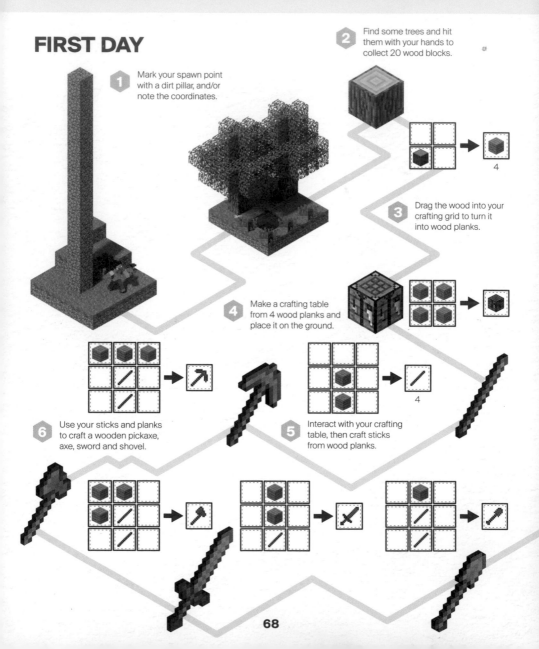

1 Mark your spawn point with a dirt pillar, and/or note the coordinates.

2 Find some trees and hit them with your hands to collect 20 wood blocks.

3 Drag the wood into your crafting grid to turn it into wood planks.

4 Make a crafting table from 4 wood planks and place it on the ground.

6 Use your sticks and planks to craft a wooden pickaxe, axe, sword and shovel.

5 Interact with your crafting table, then craft sticks from wood planks.

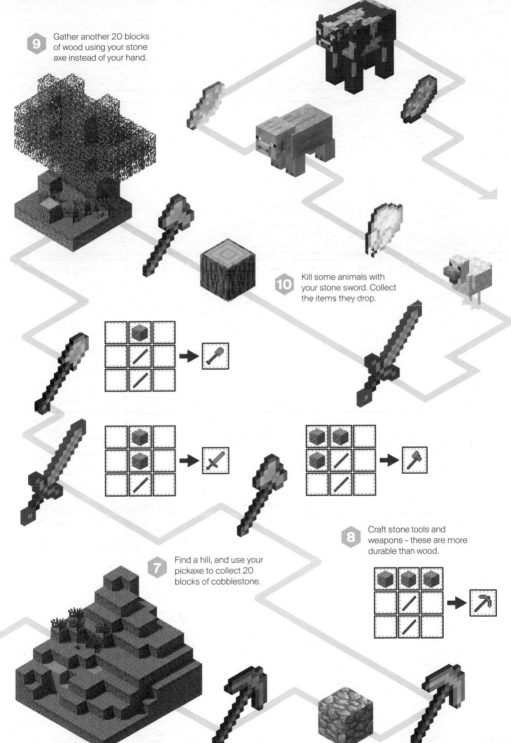

9 Gather another 20 blocks of wood using your stone axe instead of your hand.

10 Kill some animals with your stone sword. Collect the items they drop.

8 Craft stone tools and weapons – these are more durable than wood.

7 Find a hill, and use your pickaxe to collect 20 blocks of cobblestone.

69

11 Kill 3 sheep, then craft a bed. This allows you to sleep through the night.

DID YOU KNOW? ↗

Didn't manage to build a shelter? Stand on a 3-block-high dirt tower until day comes so hostile mobs can't reach you. You could also dig 3 blocks straight down, jump in and place a block over your head until morning. Put a torch on the wall so you're not stuck in darkness.

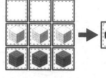

12 Craft a furnace. This allows you to smelt items into more useful forms.

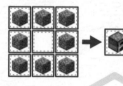

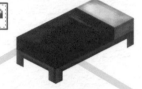

14 Eat the cooked meat when your food bar starts to go down. (See pages 74-75.)

13 Use your wooden tools as fuel to cook the raw meat (you don't need them now).

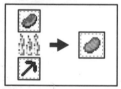

15 Go back to the hill, and dig farther in until you spot some coal ore.

16 Mine as many blocks of coal ore as you can – each will drop 1 coal.

DID YOU KNOW? ↗

No coal ore in sight? Charcoal can be used instead of coal to make torches. Place wood in both furnace slots to create charcoal.

21 Light up your hole using torches to prevent hostile mobs spawning overnight. Shut the door and either sleep in your bed or wait until morning. Hide round the corner, out of sight of the door.

MOJANG STUFF

First day too easy for you? Try something like The 404 Challenge, which became really popular in the early days of Minecraft. The name refers to the world seed number 404, which spawns you on a large gravel plane with a huge cave just beneath the surface. You have a day to collect resources above ground, then, survive the night inside the cave!

20 Craft a wooden door and place it on your shelter from the outside.

DID YOU KNOW?

If you don't manage to make a bed before sunset, use the night to cook any raw food and craft more equipment (see the next page for ideas). You could also start mining beneath your shelter if you're feeling brave ...

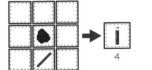

3

19 Expand the hole into an L-shape shelter, so you can hide round the corner.

18 Now you can use coal in your furnace – it'll smelt more items.

17 Craft torches. These can be placed on other blocks to provide light.

4

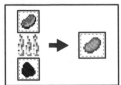

YOUR SECOND DAY

Congratulations – you've made it to day two! Now's the time to fill your inventory with supplies, deal with any resilient hostile mobs that are still lurking and craft more items. Here are some useful crafting recipes to get you started.

CHEST

A chest has 27 slots and is used to store blocks and items. Place two single chests next to each other in your shelter to create a double chest, and transfer materials from your inventory to free up some valuable space.

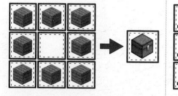

LADDER

Ladders help you ascend and descend quickly and safely. They come in handy when you encounter steep cliffs and when you start mining deeper into the ground. Just place them on the side of the blocks you wish to climb.

BOAT

Boats allow you to travel across water more quickly – they're a great investment if you live near an ocean and will be essential when the time comes for you to explore new biomes further from home.

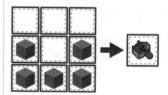

MOJANG STUFF

Pick up a chest and its contents will spill out onto the ground. If you want to carry your stuff around with you, craft a shulker box from shulker shells and a chest.

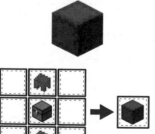

TRAPDOOR

If you start a mine underneath your base it's a good idea to place a trapdoor on the entrance to prevent hostile mobs from coming up. You'll need to attach the trapdoor to the block to the side of your entrance.

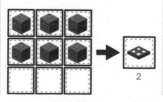

BOWL

You'll need a bowl if you want to cook rabbit stew, mushroom stew or beetroot soup. See pages 76-77 for more information. Bowls can also be used on mooshrooms for instant mushroom stew.

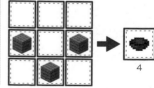

IRON ORE

Your next priority is to find iron ore, which can be smelted into iron ingots and used to make a variety of tools and weapons. Iron ore can be found at sea level and below, in veins of up to 8 blocks. Look out for orange flecks amongst the cobblestone, then mine as many blocks as you can with your stone pickaxe. Once mined you'll need to smelt iron ore in your furnace to make usable iron ingots, then use it in the crafting recipes below.

IRON TOOLS AND WEAPONS

Upgrade your tools and weapons – use the recipes on page 69 but replace the stone with iron ingots.

IRON ORE

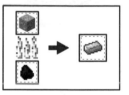

DID YOU KNOW? ↗

You can make gold and diamond tools and weapons – replace the iron ingots with gold ingots or diamonds. Gold equipment wears out quickly but is the easiest to enchant, and diamond equipment is the most durable. See pages 86-87 for tips on how to find gold and diamond.

IRON DOOR

Unlike a wooden door, zombies will never be able to break down an iron door. They're more complicated than wooden doors, though, so you'll need to place buttons on the inside and outside to activate them.

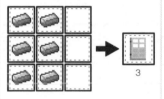

3

BUCKET

Buckets are tools that allow you to pick up and carry water and lava. You can then place the contents in a new location. Buckets can also be used to milk cows and mooshrooms.

FLINT AND STEEL

Flint and steel creates fire when used on top of a solid block. You'll need it to light TNT and Nether portals. It's crafted from an iron ingot and flint (sometimes dropped by gravel). See page 55 for the TNT recipe.

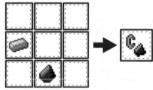

SHEARS

Shears can be used to remove wool from sheep without killing them – and there'll be more of it if you shear rather than kill them. Shears also come in handy when exploring jungle biomes as they quickly destroy leaves.

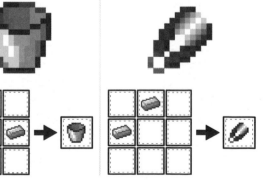

HEALTH AND FOOD

In Survival mode you'll need to keep an eye on your health and food bars, which sit just above your hotbar. It's important to eat frequently and heal when you take damage, otherwise your health bar will reach zero and you'll die.

HEALTH POINTS

When you first spawn in Survival mode you'll have a full 20 health points (10 hearts) and a full 20 food points (10 shanks). As you play, you'll take damage, use energy and lose points. To restore your health points you'll need to eat and avoid taking damage for a while. Your food bar shows you how hungry you are – when it's full you won't be able to eat any more.

You lose health points through:

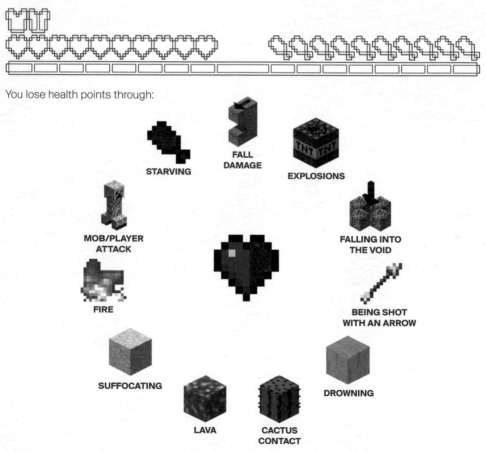

STARVING

FALL DAMAGE

EXPLOSIONS

MOB/PLAYER ATTACK

FALLING INTO THE VOID

FIRE

BEING SHOT WITH AN ARROW

SUFFOCATING

DROWNING

LAVA

CACTUS CONTACT

You lose health points rapidly during combat so it's a good idea to keep food in a hotbar slot. Different types of food restore different amounts of food points – read on for details.

**RAW
BEEF**
3 food points

 STEAK
8 food points

 **RAW
PORK CHOP**
3 food points

**COOKED
PORK CHOP**
8 food points

 **RAW
CHICKEN**
2 food points

**ROAST
CHICKEN**
6 food points

**RAW
MUTTON**
2 food points

**COOKED
MUTTON**
6 food points

**RAW
RABBIT**
3 food points

**COOKED
RABBIT**
5 food points

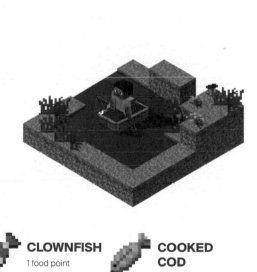

MEAT

Most animals drop raw meat when they die. This meat will be cooked if they were killed by fire. Meat is an excellent food source as it restores more food points than fruit and vegetables. Cooked meat restores more food points than raw meat.

FISH

If you have a fishing rod and access to water, raw fish are an unlimited resource and an excellent food source. Raw fish can also be obtained by defeating polar bears and guardians (see pages 49 and 58-59). Cooking fish in a furnace will increase its food points. Use your fishing rod to cast it into the water. When the bobber dips, reel it back in to see what you've caught.

TIP

Fishing doesn't just catch you fish – there's a probability that you'll get junk items and, occasionally, really valuable items like enchanted books. You can put enchantments on your fishing rod, too – that'll increase your chance of snagging the good stuff.

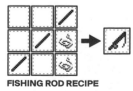
FISHING ROD RECIPE

 CLOWNFISH
1 food point

 **COOKED
COD**
5 food points

**RAW
COD**
2 food points

**COOKED
SALMON**
6 food points

**RAW
SALMON**
2 food points

FRUIT AND VEGETABLES

Fruit and vegetables don't restore as many food points as meat, but they are a good alternative if you can't find any animals. They are readily available all over the Overworld, if you know where to look, and several can be crafted into more useful items.

 Potatoes can be found in village farms, and zombies occasionally drop potatoes when they die. A potato can be baked in a furnace to increase its food points.

A potato restores 1 food point, a baked potato restores 5 food points.

Beetroot can be found in NPC village farms. It can be eaten immediately or crafted into beetroot soup.

Beetroot restores 1 food point, beetroot soup restores 6 food points.

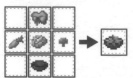

RABBIT STEW RECIPE

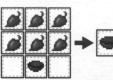

BEETROOT SOUP RECIPE

 Carrots can be found in village farms. Zombies occasionally drop carrots when they die.

Restores 3 food points.

Apples can be obtained by destroying oak and dark oak leaves, and can be found in naturally generated chests. Villagers may also sell apples for emeralds.

Restores 4 food points.

5 In addition to restoring food points, a golden apple provides an effect known as 'absorption I' which absorbs damage for 2 minutes, as well as 'regeneration II' which heals damage for 5 seconds. Golden apples can be found in naturally generated chests.

Restores 4 food points.

GOLDEN APPLE RECIPE

6 Mushroom stew can be obtained by 'milking' a mooshroom with a bowl, and can be crafted.

Restores 6 food points.

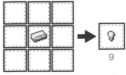

MUSHROOM STEW RECIPE

7 In addition to restoring food points, a golden carrot restores 14 saturation (your food bar starts to decline when your saturation reaches 0) and can be used in brewing potions. You'll need gold nuggets to craft one.

Restores 6 food points.

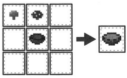

GOLDEN NUGGET RECIPE

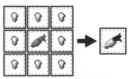

GOLDEN CARROT RECIPE

8 3-7 melon slices can be obtained by mining melon blocks, found in jungle biomes.

Each melon slice restores 2 food points.

BAKED GOODS

With the right ingredients you can craft a variety of more complex 'baked' goods to top up your food points and add a little variety to your diet. Here's a quick guide to locating and collecting the necessary items.

1 Gather wheat from NPC village farms or from dungeon, igloo or woodland mansion chests. It can also be found in dungeon and igloo chests.

Bread can be found in naturally generated chests. Villager farmers will sell 2-4 bread for an emerald.

Restores 5 food points.

BREAD RECIPE

2 Sugar cane is often found near water. Harvest some, then place it in your crafting grid to make sugar.

SUGAR RECIPE

BASE INGREDIENTS

1   2   3   4   5   6

3 Milk can be obtained by using a bucket on a cow.

4 Pumpkins spawn randomly on grass blocks across the Overworld.

Villager farmers will sell 2-3 pumpkin pies for an emerald.

Restores 8 food points.

PUMPKIN PIE RECIPE

5 Eggs are laid by chickens and can be found all over the Overworld.

Villager farmers sell 1 cake for 1 emerald. Cake must be placed on another block before it can be eaten. A cake has 7 slices, and each time you click on a cake with the 'use item' button you will eat 1 slice.

Restores 2 food points per slice – 14 food points total.

Villager farmers will sell 6 cookies for an emerald.

Restores 2 food points.

6 Cocoa beans can be harvested from cocoa growing on the side of jungle trees.

COOKIE RECIPE

CAKE RECIPE

79

SETTING UP YOUR OWN FARM

Although you can find sources of food throughout the Overworld, life will be a lot easier if you set up a crop and animal farm next to your shelter. That way you'll have a sustainable source of food right on your doorstep.

BREEDING ANIMALS

As you know, animals have many uses, so an animal farm is a profitable investment. You'll need to stock up on the food each animal responds to, then build a pen and lead them inside to breed.

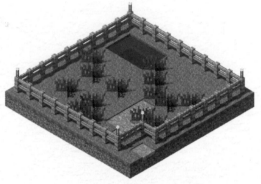

1 Choose a suitable grassy spot for your pen, near to your shelter. It should be at least 10 x 10 blocks and well-lit to prevent hostile mobs spawning inside.

WOOD FENCE RECIPE

2 Hunt some animals. If you have string and slime, craft leads so you can easily manoeuvre the animals into the pen. If not, lead two of each animal into the pen by holding the food item they respond to.

LEAD RECIPE

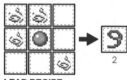

3 Feed two of the same animal when they are within 8 blocks of each other and they will enter love mode. After a moment a baby animal will appear.

FOODS FOR BREEDING

RABBIT
Dandelions
Carrots
Golden carrots

PIG
Carrots
Potatoes
Beetroot

HORSE
Golden apples
Golden carrots

SHEEP
Wheat

CAT
Raw cod
Raw salmon
Clownfish
Pufferfish

COW
Wheat

MOOSHROOM
Wheat

TAMED WOLF
Any raw meat
Any cooked meat

LLAMA
Hay bales

CHICKEN
Seeds
Pumpkin seeds
Melon seeds
Beetroot seeds

TIP

Bored of white wool? You can dye your
sheep before breeding them to create
more coloured sheep. The baby sheep
will be the colour of one of its parents,
or it will be a combination, if the colours
can mix. Many flowers can be used
as dyes, as well as cactus, lapis lazuli,
cocoa beans and ink sacs.

CROP FARMING

Different crops require different conditions to grow, and it's important to create the right environment. Choose a flat area of dirt, then follow the steps below to create a crop farm.

CARROTS, POTATOES, BEETROOT AND WHEAT

1 Collect carrots, potatoes, beetroot and wheat from village farms. Wheat seeds can also be collected by destroying tall grass.

2 Craft a hoe – you'll need this to till dirt blocks into farmland.

IRON HOE RECIPE

3 Create a single water source block in the middle of your chosen area, then use your hoe to till a 9 x 9 area around it.

4 Surround your farm with fences and a gate to protect it from hungry animals.

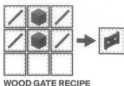

WOOD GATE RECIPE

5 Place torches around the edges to provide a light source at night (these crops need light to grow).

6 Plant your crops, then wait for them to reach full maturity. If you harvest them before they reach full maturity they will only drop seeds. Replant some of each harvest to keep your farm going.

TIP ↗

Bone meal is a fantastic fertiliser. Use it on your crops to bring them to full maturity immediately.

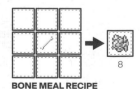

8

BONE MEAL RECIPE

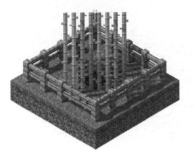

SUGAR CANE

Sugar cane must be planted on dirt, grass or sand that is right next to a water block. It doesn't need light to grow. You'll need sugar cane to make sugar for baking and paper for making books for bookcases. (Bookcases will come in useful when you start enchanting items.)

> **TIP** ↗
>
> When harvesting fully mature sugar cane (3 blocks high), aim for the middle block so you don't have to replant it.

MELONS AND PUMPKINS

Melons and pumpkins don't need water to grow – just farmland. Till some dirt and make sure there's a block of space to the side, then plant melon or pumpkin seeds. A stem will grow, eventually producing a melon or pumpkin in the adjacent block. When you harvest the melon/pumpkin, the stem will remain and the growth process will begin again.

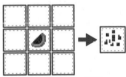 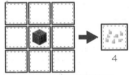

MELON SEEDS RECIPE **PUMPKIN SEEDS RECIPE**

Melon seeds can be crafted from melon slices, and can sometimes be found in chests.

Pumpkin seeds can be crafted from a pumpkin, and can sometimes be found in chests.

MUSHROOMS

Mushrooms only grow in areas where the light level is 12 or lower, unless planted on mycelium or podzol (podzol is a type of dirt found exclusively in taiga biomes). Once planted, mushrooms will spread to nearby blocks that meet their light requirement, as long as there aren't more than 4 mushrooms of that type in a 9 x 9 area.

MYCELIUM   **PODZOL**

83

MINING

Mining is a tricky business, but it's essential if you want to get your hands on rare and useful materials. Many of the rarest items are found beneath the surface of your world, and can only be mined with certain tools.

THE GOLDEN RULES

Follow these golden rules to stay safe as you descend below ground and ensure you return to the surface laden with the supplies you need.

1 Prepare your inventory. You'll need wood to craft more tools underground, and coal for torches. You'll also need plenty of food to keep your health bar full.

2 Never dig straight up or straight down. This is Minecraft's number one rule – if you mine the block directly below your feet you could fall into lava or into a cave full of hostile mobs. If you dig directly above your head you could find yourself engulfed in a lava stream, drowning in water or suffocating in sand or gravel.

3 Leave a trail of torches as you descend, to help you find the way out. Always place them on the same side.

4 Find a naturally generated cave system which will lead you deep underground and save you a lot of digging.

5 Use the sneak function when walking along ledges – this stops you falling off the edge. Check pages 8-10 for a reminder of how to do this on your Edition.

6 Keep a water bucket in your hotbar, so you can quickly put yourself out if you do accidentally fall into lava.

7 Use your ears. If you hear running water or bubbling lava, be careful. A squeaking bat signals a cavern is nearby.

8 Take a stack of ladders to help you ascend back to the surface quickly and safely.

MINING FOR ORES

Minecraft's most valuable blocks are found deep underground, near the bottom of the world. Rare ores generate below level 32, where hostile mobs spawn freely in the dark and lava is a serious hazard. You'll need an iron pickaxe or better to mine most ores.

TIP

The best level at which to mine for ores is y=10 to y=15 since all ores generate within this band. Remember to check your coordinates as you descend.

SEA LEVEL

62

49

IRON ORE

48

33

COAL ORE

GOLD ORE

Found in veins of 4-8 blocks, at layer 32 and under, gold ore drops itself when mined. You'll need to smelt it in a furnace to turn it into gold ingots. Gold can be used to craft armour, tools and weapons as well as golden apples, clocks and powered rails.

REDSTONE ORE

Redstone ore is found in veins of 4-8 blocks, at layer 16 and under. When mined, each block drops 4-5 redstone. Redstone can be used like a wire to transmit power, and to craft various items e.g. clocks, compasses and powered rails.

LAPIS LAZULI ORE

Lapis lazuli ore is found in veins of 1-10 blocks, at layer 31 and under. When mined with a stone pickaxe or better, each block drops 4-8 pieces of lapis lazuli. Lapis lazuli can be used in enchanting and as a dye.

DIAMOND ORE

Found in veins of 1-10 blocks, at layer 16 and under, each block of diamond ore will drop 1 diamond. Diamonds can be used to craft the most durable tools, weapons and armour, as well as jukeboxes and enchantment tables.

32

17

16

0

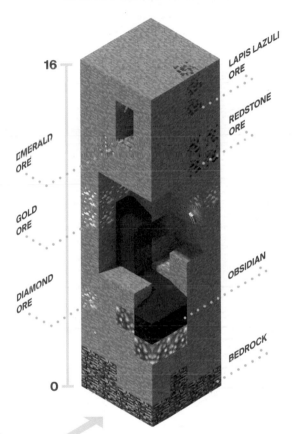

LAPIS LAZULI ORE

REDSTONE ORE

EMERALD ORE

GOLD ORE

DIAMOND ORE

OBSIDIAN

BEDROCK

EMERALD ORE

Found in single blocks between layers 4 and 32 in extreme hills biomes, emerald ore drops 1 emerald when mined. Emeralds can be used in villager trading. See page 47 for more info. They can also be crafted into decorative blocks of emerald.

DID YOU KNOW?

Obsidian is often found towards the bottom of the world where flowing water hits a lava source. It's the toughest mineable block in Survival mode, and is the only block that can only be mined with a diamond pickaxe. You'll need it to make a Nether portal and an enchantment table.

COMBAT

Unless you choose the peaceful option, Survival mode requires you to fight for your life. Pro Minecrafters use potions and enchantments to improve their performance, but here's a guide to basic combat to get you started.

BASIC COMBAT

You'll need a few key items to defend yourself from hostile mobs or enemy players. These crafting recipes will give you a fighting chance.

Craft a wood, stone, iron, gold or diamond sword and hit your opponent to inflict damage.

An axe does more damage per hit than a sword, but takes longer to recover.

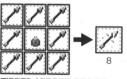
SHIELD RECIPE

A shield allows you to block attacks, reducing the damage you take, but you'll slow to sneaking pace.

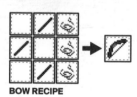
BOW RECIPE

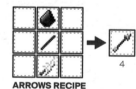
ARROWS RECIPE

4

You can attack hostile mobs or enemy players from a safe distance with a bow and arrows.

MOJANG STUFF

Jump a moment before swinging your weapon to perform a critical strike that does 50% more damage than a regular hit.

DID YOU KNOW?

You'll need string to craft a bow. Spiders may drop string when they die, but abandoned mineshafts are also a great source of string since they're home to cave spiders. Just find some cobwebs and break them with a sword.

TIPPED ARROWS RECIPE

8

Tipped arrows are arrows that have been combined with potions and administer the potion's effect upon contact. You can brew potions and they are sometimes dropped by witches when they die.

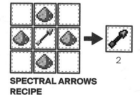
SPECTRAL ARROWS RECIPE

2

Spectral arrows give the glowing effect for 10 seconds, so your target is visible even through solid blocks. Glowstone dust can be found in the Nether and is sometimes dropped by witches.

ARMOUR

To help protect yourself from damage you can craft a full set of armour – a helmet, chestplate, trousers and boots – from 24 units of leather, iron, gold or diamond. Each substance gives you a different level of protection: leather is the weakest, and diamond is the strongest.

DID YOU KNOW?

Equip a pumpkin in your helmet slot to wear it on your head. This will come in handy when you encounter endermen – see page 51 for more details.

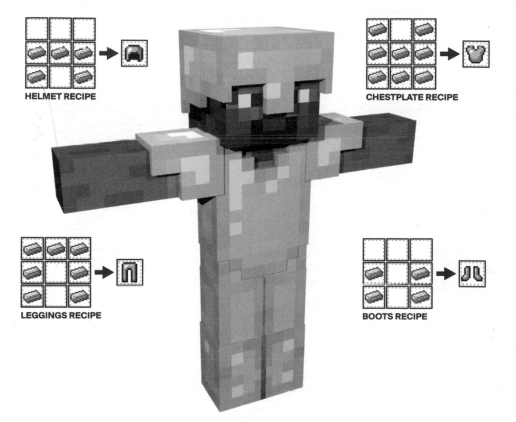

HELMET RECIPE

CHESTPLATE RECIPE

LEGGINGS RECIPE

BOOTS RECIPE

Once you've crafted your armour, open your inventory and locate the four armour slots. Equip your armour here and it will appear on your body, and an armour bar will appear above your health points. Keep an eye on it to check how much durability is left – it will decrease as the armour absorbs damage, and eventually you'll need to craft a new set or repair on an anvil.

ARMOUR WILL PROTECT AGAINST:

UPGRADE YOUR SHELTER

So all that mining and mob combat paid off and your inventory is packed with useful blocks and items just waiting to be used. Now it's time to upgrade your shelter so you have a secure base from which to prepare for your next adventure.

1 Expand your shelter by digging further into your cliff face and/or moving your outer walls. Replace any dirt with cobblestone.

2 Install glass windows so you can see what's happening outside your shelter without having to open your door.

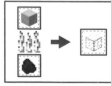

GLASS RECIPE

3 Craft more furnaces and chests to make the most of the space inside your shelter. Organise your chests so you store similar items together.

4 Add more torches around your shelter to reduce the number of hostile mobs that spawn on your doorstep.

5 Build a perimeter wall with an overhang to stop spiders climbing over. Iron bars topped with stone slabs are ideal.

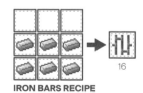

IRON BARS RECIPE

16

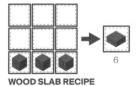

STONE SLAB RECIPE

6

WOOD SLAB RECIPE

6

NAVIGATING

There's a whole world waiting to be explored beyond the horizon
- exciting new biomes full of resources and rare loot, and mobs
you've never seen before. It's easy to get lost on long journeys, so
make sure you're prepared before you set off.

1 Mark your shelter with a beacon
and remember to make a note of
your coordinates to help you find
your way back.

2 A compass will point to your
spawn point, which will help you
get back home if you built your
shelter nearby.

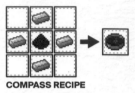

COMPASS RECIPE

3 A map shows you what's in the
immediate area and will help
you decide which way you'd
like to go.

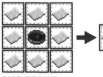

MAP RECIPE

6 Prepare your inventory with plenty of food, tools and weapons to sustain you on your travels.

5 It's easy to get lost in Minecraft, so craft signs and torches and use them to mark a trail back to your shelter.

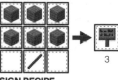

SIGN RECIPE

4 A clock shows the position of the sun and moon and is handy when you're underground and want to know if it's day or night.

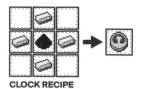

CLOCK RECIPE

FINAL WORDS

Congratulations! You've made it to the end of our Guide to Exploration. Remember everything you've read and you'll be a master crafter capable of surviving anything the Overworld throws at you, and the perils of the Nether and beyond. Thanks for playing!

OWEN JONES
THE MOJANG TEAM

STAY IN THE KNOW!

GUIDE TO: ☑CREATIVE

GUIDE TO: ☑EXPLORATION

GUIDE TO: ☑ THE NETHER & THE END

GUIDE TO: ☑REDSTONE

MINECRAFT MOBESTIARY

AN ILLUSTRATED GUIDE TO THE MOBS OF MINECRAFT

MINECRAFT MEDIEVAL FORTRESS

BUILDS

MINECRAFT

THE SURVIVORS' BOOK OF SECRETS

Learn about the latest Minecraft books

when you sign up for our newsletter at

RANDOMHOUSEBOOKS.COM/MINECRAFT

DEL REY